Five reasons why you'll love Isadora Moon...

Meet the magical, fang-tastic Isadora Moon!

Isadora's cuddly toy, Pink Rabbit, has been magicked to life!

Isadora is having a sleepover with mermaids!

Isadora's family is crazy!

Enchanting pink and black pictures

What fun things would you get up to at a mermaid sleepover?

I'd learn mermaid hula hooping. - Poppy

We'd explore a shipwreck and a cave full of seaweed! - Maggie

We'd have a midnight feast and eat a beautiful rainbow pie. - Jas

I'd learn how to swim
loop the loops! - Blue

We'd make shell
necklaces and I would
flick my tail. - Rosa

I'd sleep in the mermaid's
bedroom, which would be
blue and pink and covered in
seashells. - Clara

Family Tree

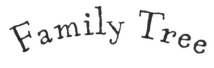

My Mum
Countess Cordelia
Moon

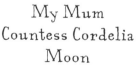

Baby Honeyblossom

My Dad
Count Bartholomew
Moon

Me!
Isadora Moon

Pink Rabbit

For vampires, fairies, and humans everywhere!
And for my sparkly Celestine.

Illustrated by Mike Garton,
based on original artwork by Harriet Muncaster

OXFORD
UNIVERSITY PRESS

Great Clarendon Street, Oxford OX2 6DP
Oxford University Press is a department of the University of Oxford.
It furthers the University's objective of excellence in research, scholarship,
and education by publishing worldwide. Oxford is a registered trade mark
of Oxford University Press in the UK and in certain other countries

Copyright © Harriet Muncaster 2022

The moral rights of the author have been asserted

Database right Oxford University Press (maker)

First published in 2022

British Library Cataloguing in Publication Data

Data available

ISBN:9780192778079

1 3 5 7 9 10 8 6 4 2

Printed in Great Britain by Bell and Bain Ltd, Glasgow

Paper used in the production of this book is a natural,
recyclable product made from wood grown in sustainable forests.
The manufacturing process conforms to the environmental
regulations of the country of origin.

MIX
Paper from
responsible sources
FSC® C007785
FSC
www.fsc.org

ISADORA · MOON

Under the Sea

Harriet Muncaster

OXFORD
UNIVERSITY PRESS

Chapter ONE

It was Saturday morning, and we were
all having breakfast in the kitchen when
suddenly there was a loud tap-tapping
on the window. It made me jump, and I
accidentally dropped my toast on the floor!
Pink Rabbit bounced onto my lap in alarm.
(Pink Rabbit used to be my favourite
stuffed toy, but my mum magicked him

alive for me with her wand. She can do
things like that because she is a fairy.)

'Bird!' shouted my baby sister
Honeyblossom from her high chair, and
she pointed her chubby little finger at
the window.

'It's a seagull,' said Mum. 'How odd! Seagulls don't usually visit our town; they live by the sea.'

'Don't let it in!' said Dad, hiding behind his vampire cape. 'It will steal my red juice! Seagulls are *notorious* for stealing food.'

My dad is a vampire, and he only eats food if it is red. He is very protective of his red juice.

'The seagull won't be interested in your red juice, Bartholomew,' said Mum, rolling her eyes fondly. 'But I think we SHOULD let it in. It's carrying something in its beak!'

'Ooh, what could it be?' I said,

hugging Pink Rabbit to my chest excitedly until he squirmed for me to let go.

Mum opened the window, and the seagull came flapping into the room. It landed in the middle of the table and dropped a letter right next to the honeypot. Dad immediately swiped his red juice away and hid it under his cape.

'It's for Isadora!' Mum exclaimed.

'Me?!' I squeaked, feeling excited and nervous all at once. Why would a seagull be bringing *me* a letter? I reached out and picked it up, tearing open the envelope. Mum, Dad, and the seagull leaned in to look.

'It's an invitation!' I said, pulling out a beautiful shell-shaped card, studded all over with glinty pearls. 'From my mermaid friend Marina. She wants me to come to her birthday sleepover next Saturday!'

'Ooh!' said Mum. 'How exciting!'

'I do hope I won't have to accompany you,' said Dad, shuddering. 'I hate getting my hair wet.'

'You don't bring your mum and dad with you to a sleepover,' I said. 'I'm supposed to go on my own!'

'On your own?!' said Dad. 'What, all that way to the sea? Under the water?'

I felt my tummy swirl with anxiety.

'I'm sure it will be very safe,' said Mum. 'Marina's parents will be there.'

I stared at the invitation. There was a little section at the bottom with a checkbox where I could tick whether I wanted to attend the party or not. I did

want to attend. But . . . it would be very
far away. Last time I went to a sleepover
I felt a little bit homesick, but it was only
a few roads away at my best friend Zoe's
house. Dad was able to visit me during his
nightly fly.

'I think you'll have a lovely time,'
said Mum. 'Marina says that she'll meet
you on the beach and give you another
magic necklace to wear so you can breathe
underwater.'

'But I won't be able to come home
easily if I want to . . .' I said.

'I'm sure you won't want to,' said
Mum. 'You'll be having too much fun!'

'Squawk!' went the seagull and tapped

his foot impatiently.

'I think he wants to get back to the beach,' said Mum, handing me a pen.

I took a deep breath and then ticked the box at the bottom of the invitation to say that I would be attending. Mum snipped it off. There—it was done! I couldn't change my mind now. I handed the section with the ticked checkbox back to the seagull who took it in his yellow beak. Then he flapped back up into the air, towards the window, swooping down to snatch up my piece of toast from the floor on his way.

'I told you!' said Dad as the seagull disappeared out of the window. '*Notorious* for stealing food!'

'Well, I think it was kind of him to fly all this way to deliver an invitation,' said Mum. 'If I'd thought of it in time, I would have magicked him up a cone of chips!'

Chapter TWO

The following week, all I could think about was the sleepover. I felt extremely excited one moment and then a bit scared the next. A sleepover! Under the sea! All on my own! By the time Saturday came around, I was feeling so full of nervous energy that I couldn't sit still. I bounced up and down on my bed with Pink Rabbit

as Mum helped to pack my suitcase.

'Calm down, Isadora,' laughed
Mum, 'or you'll have no energy for the
party! Now, do you want to bring your
swimming costume with you or your
pyjamas? I'm unsure which would be best
for this sort of sleepover. And don't forget
Marina's present. Why don't you go and
wrap it up right now? I bought some
waterproof paper for you to use.'

After we had eaten lunch, it was time to go! Mum, Dad, Honeyblossom, and I got into the car. Dad usually sleeps throughout the day, but he had stayed up specially for the trip.

'I want to see you off!' he said as he got into the passenger seat. 'But I *am* going to have forty winks while Mum drives.' Then he popped in his earplugs, pulled his sleep mask down over his eyes, and started snoring.

It felt like a long drive down to the coast. I stared out of the window as the roads changed from being motorways to little country lanes. Eventually, I spotted a line of sparkling blue on the horizon.

'The sea!' sang Mum happily. 'The beautiful sea!'

Pink Rabbit wiggled his ears in excitement.

I felt my tummy lurch as we turned down a bumpy lane and into the beach car park.

'Are we here?' asked Dad blearily, lifting up his sleep mask.

'Yes!' said Mum. 'And isn't it wonderful? Oh, I do love nature! The beach is just down that little sandy path, look!'

We all got out of the car, and Dad carried my suitcase for me as we made our way down the little path. Mum skipped ahead with Honeyblossom in her arms. Fairies love being outdoors in the sunshine!

The beach was big and very beautiful with tall cliffs and lots of dark caves and rock pools. A few humans were sitting on the sand. I knew we needed to get to a spot where no one would see a mermaid

popping out of the water. Mermaids don't really trust humans. Marina had drawn me a little map on the invitation. I got it out and studied it.

'Looks like there's a private cove past those cliffs,' said Mum, peering over my shoulder at the map. 'That's where Marina will meet us.'

We all walked towards the cliffs at the far side of the beach, where there was a cave that went right through to another, smaller beach on the other side. We walked through it and I marvelled at how dark, drippy, and echoey it felt compared to the bright sunshine outside. I wasn't scared though. I am half vampire!

'Here we are!' said Mum when we reached the beach on the other side. 'No humans! Let's have a picnic while we wait for Marina.'

Mum put down the rug, and Dad put up his big gothic umbrella to sit under. Vampires do not like the sun!

'Lovely!' said Mum.

I helped Honeyblossom to build a
sandcastle while I kept one eye on the sea.
My tummy still felt all swirly. The sea
looked so big with its rolling waves and
crashing white foam.

I was just putting a pearly pink shell on top of the sandcastle when I saw something move among the waves in the sea. I jumped up and ran towards the shoreline. It was Marina! She had popped her head up above the water and she was waving. Ocea, her pet seahorse, was beside her.

'Hello, Isadora!' she cried. 'I'm so glad you could come to my party!'

Marina looked so pleased and excited to see me that I forgot all about being nervous.

'I've brought you another seashell necklace,' said Marina, swimming closer. 'Catch!'

She threw the necklace at me, and I flew up in the air on my vampire fairy bat wings to catch it. I put it round my neck, feeling the tingly mermaid magic.

'Here's your suitcase, Isadora,' said Dad, holding it out to me. 'I hope you have a lovely time.'

'I'm sure you will,' said Mum,

giving me a big hug. 'We'll be back here tomorrow morning to pick you up.'

'OK!' I nodded.

Mum, Dad, and Honeyblossom stood and watched as I stepped into the water, feeling the cold waves lap around my ankles. Pink Rabbit clung to my neck. He hates getting wet as it takes so long for him to dry out.

'Let me make him a magic mermaid bubble, like last time,' said Marina. She splashed her tail in the water to make

some froth and then lifted one of the tiny bubbles up on the tip of her finger. She blew on it, and the bubble got bigger and bigger until it was big enough for Pink Rabbit to pop inside. Then she held out her hand to me.

'Come on,' she said. 'I can't wait for you to meet my friends!'

With one last glance at Mum, Dad, and Honeyblossom, I walked into the waves and dipped my head beneath them.

Chapter THREE

It was a cool, aqua world below. Seaweed fronds waved with the tide, and the sand shimmered under the rippling surface of the water. Marina and I swam away from the shore, towards the sapphire blue deep. We passed fish of all colours and sizes, crabs, clams, jellyfish, and squid. Some of them were quite big, and at times, I felt a little afraid, but Marina squeezed my hand.

'The sea creatures will never harm you while you're with me,' she said.

We swam on, deeper and deeper until I started to see mermaid houses built on the sand. They were smooth and curvy, with roofs made from giant twirly pointed shells. Some of them were studded all over with beautiful shimmery pearls. The further we swam, the more houses appeared, until there were whole streets of them! We were in a mermaid city! And in the distance, I could see the royal palace with its spires and turrets, like a giant sandcastle. Everything looked so pretty and magical that I couldn't stop staring.

'This is the centre of town,' said Marina, leading me down a wide street and through some swirly arches. Here there were lots of mer-people swimming about, their tails glinting and flashing all colours of the rainbow. Some were sitting outside cafes eating and drinking strange-looking cakes and smoothies. Some swam in and out of shops, carrying bags made from fishing nets. Everything glowed and twinkled with pearly light.

Marina turned off the main street and onto a side street, where there was a row of pastel-coloured shell houses.

'That's where I live!' she said, pointing to the pale aqua one.

She led me through a garden gate, and we
swam up a little path through seagrass
and ruby red anemones. The front door
opened before we even reached it.

'Isadora Moon!' said Marina's mum. 'How lovely to see you again! You're the first to arrive!'

I followed Marina into the house. It was decorated all over with glittery green and blue streamers that waved in the underwater current.

'Come up to my bedroom,' said Marina. 'I'll show you where we're going to sleep!'

She swished through a hole in the ceiling in a flurry of bubbles.

'I suppose mermaids don't need stairs,' I whispered to Pink Rabbit as we swam after her.

Marina's bedroom was big, and there

were six clamshell beds set up in a row
on the floor. They had comfy-looking
mattresses made of sea sponge and soft
seaweedy blankets. I put my suitcase next
to the one nearest the window just as the
doorbell rang.

'Ooh!' said Marina. 'More guests!'

And she swished out of the room, leaving
Pink Rabbit and me on our own. I
suddenly felt a bit nervous again. I didn't
know any of Marina's mermaid friends. I
busied myself with unzipping my suitcase
and putting my pyjamas beneath the
pillow of my clamshell bed. After a few

moments, I heard laughing and giggling, and in a swoosh of bubbles, two mermaids came into the bedroom with Marina. I recognized one of the mermaids. It was Princess Delphina! I had met her once before. She was clutching her special mer-bear to her chest—the very same one I had magicked alive for her with my wand.

'Isadora!' said Delphina. 'How nice to see you again! How are you? This is my sister, Emerald.' She pointed to a mermaid with pale aqua skin, spiky black hair, and fins coming out from the side of her head. She looked very different to Delphina. She also looked a little bit grumpy because she only gave me a half-smile and then went

to put her bag down on the clamshell bed next to mine.

'I didn't know you had a sister, Delphina,' I said.

'I didn't until recently,' said Delphina. 'But my dad, the king, got married again a few months ago to a merlady called Coral. Coral is Emerald's mum, so now we're sisters!'

She beamed, but I noticed that Emerald didn't look so happy.

Just then the doorbell rang again, and Marina disappeared from the room for a few moments. I suddenly felt a bit shy and unsure of what to say. But Marina soon came back with two more friends—a mermaid and a merboy.

'This is Oceana and Finn,' said
Marina, introducing them to me.
'Everyone, this is Isadora Moon. She's a
vampire fairy.'

They both looked so friendly that my shyness immediately evaporated.

'A vampire fairy?' asked Oceana wonderingly. 'Ooh! What's it like to live on land, Isadora?'

'Oh, well . . .' I began, pleased to be asked a question. I started to tell all the merfriends about my family and my human school. They were all very interested. All except Emerald, who just sat on her clamshell bed with her back to us, petting Ocea the seahorse.

After we had finished talking, Marina's mum called us downstairs for games and party food. We played swim through the hoop, pass the parcel, and

sleeping flatfish. Then Marina opened her
presents. She got a beautiful music box
made of shells from Delphina, a cuddly
toy jellyfish from Oceana, a pearly collar
for her pet seahorse from Finn, and a
clamshell locket necklace from Emerald.

I gave her a book which Mum had used her fairy magic on to make the pages waterproof. It was all about my favourite ballet dancer, Tatiana Tutu.

'How fascinating!' said Marina's mum, coming over to have a look. 'It's always important to learn about other people's worlds.'

'Having legs must feel so weird,' said Delphina. 'I just can't imagine how it would feel to *dance*!'

'I can't imagine having a tail,' I said. 'And being able to *swish*!'

We all laughed, and then Marina's mum said it was time for tea. There was a big table set up with all kinds of party food on it that I had never seen before. There were seaweed scones and seaberry cupcakes and bowls of greeny-blue jelly with sugar pearl sprinkles. It was delicious—if a little soggy. As I ate, I looked around the table at Marina and all her merfriends.

It felt so nice to have been invited to the party. I was having such a nice time so far that I wasn't missing Mum or Dad even a tiny bit! Everyone seemed happy. Even Emerald was smiling *slightly* now that she had a bowl of jelly in front of her.

After tea, Marina's mum got out loads of beautiful shells and glittering jewels.

'Who wants to make a shell crown?' she asked.

'ME!' we all cried.

I LOVED making my shell crown. I spent ages on it, making sure that it was as shimmery and sparkly as possible. There were even enough shells for me to make a little one for Pink Rabbit too.

I glanced across the table to see what everyone else had made. Oceana's crown was detailed and delicate, with silver seaweed swirls. Marina's was all different shades of pink, and Delphina's was . . . very similar to the one Emerald was making, which was black and spiky and gothic, with shiny green gems dotted all over it. Delphina was copying everything that Emerald was doing. I wondered why. A black spiky crown didn't seem very . . . Delphina.

Suddenly Emerald looked up and noticed what was going on. She frowned.

'You're copying me!' she said.

'I know!' said Delphina excitedly.
'As we're sisters now, I thought we should
have matching crowns!'

She beamed at Emerald, but Emerald
scowled back.

'I don't want to have matching
crowns,' she said. 'And I *don't* want to be
sisters!'

'But . . .' said Delphina, her face

falling.

'Just leave me alone, Delphina!' said
Emerald, turning away and hunching over
so that Delphina couldn't copy any more
of her crown.

We all stared at Delphina and each
other in shock. Delphina's face had gone
very white. She gulped, and I could tell
that she was swallowing down tears. I
felt very sorry for her, and I decided that
I didn't really like Emerald at all. What a
mean mermaid!

Oceana swam round the table and put
her arm around Delphina.

'That wasn't very nice, Emerald,' she
said.

Emerald just shrugged and carried on making her crown in private. She didn't join in with anyone else for the rest of the crown-making session, and I started to wonder why Marina had invited her to the party. She didn't seem like a very nice friend.

Chapter FOUR

It had started to get dark by the time
we finished our crowns, so we all went
up to Marina's room to get ready for
bed. Delphina had cheered up and was
laughing and chatting with us all. But I
noticed that she didn't say anything else to
Emerald and chose the bed furthest away
from her. We all went into the bathroom

to brush our teeth except Emerald, who was busy rooting around in her suitcase. I decided to put my pyjamas on, even though I was the only one who did so.

'Mermaids don't need to wear pyjamas, I suppose!' I said to Pink Rabbit, as we snuggled down together in our shell bed. I slightly regretted picking the bed next to the window now as Emerald had picked the one next to me, and all the other merfriends seemed further away. I couldn't easily join in with their whispering, which went on for ages and ages after Marina's mum turned out the lights. And, of course, Emerald didn't join in. She just curled up in a tight ball and ignored everyone. It made me feel just the tiniest bit homesick. I wriggled down underneath the blanket, hugging Pink Rabbit tightly through his magic bubble.

'Let's try and stay awake for a midnight feast!' came Oceana's voice through the darkness.

'Of course!' said Delphina sleepily.

'We can eat the leftover party food,' Marina said, yawning. 'Everyone, try and stay awake!'

'I'll tell a ghost story!' said Finn. 'It's about an old abandoned shipwreck . . .'

But even though the merfriends all tried their hardest to stay awake, one by one they stopped whispering and drifted off to sleep until I was sure that I was the only one still awake. I lay there and gazed out of the window. It felt strange not to see the starry night sky, as I did from my

bedroom at home. Instead, small glowy
fish kept darting past the window against
the inky black of the
deep sea. I shivered and
cuddled Pink Rabbit
closer.

Now that it was dark and quiet, my mind kept thinking about how far under the sea I actually was. Miles and miles away from Mum, Dad, and Honeyblossom. It made me feel a bit funny, and my heart began to pound a little faster. What if my magic necklace stopped working? What if somehow Marina forgot the way back to the beach tomorrow? Scary thoughts kept tumbling into my head, making me feel more and more frightened and alone, when suddenly I heard a little snuffling sound from the clamshell bed next to me. It sounded like Emerald was still awake!

'Sniff.'

I frowned into the darkness. Was

Emerald OK? It sounded a little bit like she was . . . crying. But I felt a bit afraid to talk to her after the way she had acted during the party today.

'*Sniff, sniff.*'

If Emerald *was* upset, I couldn't just ignore her!

'Emerald,' I whispered. 'Are you OK?'

She didn't reply.

Forgetting all about my own worries, I sat up in bed and lit my wand. Emerald was curled up in bed with her eyes tightly closed, looking crosser and sadder than ever.

'What's wrong?' I asked, slipping out

of my bed and kneeling by hers to give her
a cuddle. I was surprised to find that she
let me.

'My dad forgot to pack my favourite
starfish plushie,' sobbed Emerald.

'Oh!' I said, surprised. Was that all?
Why had Emerald not mentioned this
earlier on when we had been getting ready

for bed? And after the way she had acted today, she didn't seem like the sort of mermaid who would be upset about going to bed without a plushie.

'I ALWAYS sleep with my starfish plushie,' said Emerald angrily. 'Dad knows that!'

She sat up in bed, her spiky black hair waving furiously about her face.

'Should we wake Marina's mum and dad and get them to call him?' I asked. 'I saw a shell phone in the entrance hall. Maybe your dad could bring the starfish plushie?'

'No,' said Emerald fiercely. 'They'll think I'm silly. And anyway, it's too late. I don't want to wake them.'

'I'm sure they wouldn't mind,' I said.

'I really don't want to bother them,' said Emerald, putting her chin on her knees and sighing.

Neither of us said anything else for a moment, and all I could hear were the soft snores of Pink Rabbit tucked up in my clamshell bed. Then suddenly Emerald sat up straighter, her eyes sparkling.

'I know what I have to do!' she said. 'I have to go to my dad's house and fetch starfish plushie myself!'

'What?!' I said. 'You can't do that! It's the middle of the night!'

'No one will know,' said Emerald.

'And Scallop City is very safe.'

I glanced out of the window at the deep, dark water.

'You can't go alone,' I said.

'I have to,' said Emerald, uncurling her tail and swishing out of the bed. 'Don't tell on me will you, Isadora? I don't want to worry anyone. I'll be back soon, I promise!'

She swam over to the window and slid it open.

'Wait!' I said, pushing down any fear. 'I think I should come with you. I want to make sure you're OK.'

'Really?' said Emerald, looking pleased.

'Yes,' I said, resolutely.

I swam over to join her at the
window, and together we slipped through
the open gap. Emerald closed it from the
other side.

'We don't want all the fish swimming
in!' she said.

We were outside Marina's house now,
floating outside her bedroom window. The
street was dark and quiet, with beautiful
swirly shell lamps glowing all along the
edges of the road.

'Where do you live, Emerald?' I asked. 'Are we going to the palace?'

'No,' said Emerald. 'That's where my *mum* lives with Delphina's dad. We're going to *my* dad's. He's the one who packed my overnight bag. He lives across town. Follow me!'

She began to swim, leading me towards the main street. It was very quiet there, and all the shops were closed, their windows glowing with magical mermaid light. Emerald swam onwards, swishing her tail in a flurry of bubbles. We went up and down so many streets that I lost track of where we were going, and I started to feel a little nervous. I think Emerald was a

bit nervous too, as she swam very fast. It was hard to keep up! Eventually, she took my hand and pulled me along until we arrived outside a small pearly pink house with roof tiles made from clamshells. The front garden was a burst of coral!

'Here we are,' said Emerald. She
swooshed right up to the front door and
banged it hard. We waited, floating in the
watery darkness. Emerald frowned.

'Why is Dad not in?' she said, crossly. 'I bet he's out with Sirena!'

'Sirena?' I asked.

'Dad's new girlfriend,' said Emerald, her eyes sparking angrily.

Suddenly everything made more sense. This was about more than just a starfish plushie.

'Don't you like Sirena?' I asked.

'I mean, she's *OK*,' said Emerald. 'But she spends so much time with Dad! And I'm sure they're keeping a secret from me. They've been whispering about something for the last few days, and they stop as soon as I come into the room. Anyway, it doesn't matter. They're not here, and there's no way in. Dad locks the windows when he goes out.'

She sat down against the front door and put her head in her hands. I sat down too and put my arm around her.

'I'm sure he didn't mean to forget the starfish plushie,' I said.

'Well, he wouldn't have forgotten if he hadn't been so busy doing something secret with Sirena this morning,' said Emerald.

We both sat in silence for a few moments, and a shoal of glowing fish passed by overhead. Emerald hung her head so that her hair covered her face and fiddled with some barnacles on the doorframe.

'I suppose we had better get back to Marina's,' I said.

'I suppose,' said Emerald. She sounded deflated.

I held out my hand and Emerald took it. We started to swim over the coral garden and away from the house. As we did so, I noticed the silhouettes of two merpeople coming towards us. I squinted into the deep dark-blue water.

Suddenly, without warning, Emerald let go of my hand and went shooting off towards the figures, leaving a stream of bubbles fizzing out behind her.

'Dad!' she shouted.

The merman came whizzing towards

us and held out his arms towards Emerald. She dive-bombed into them and burst into tears.

'Emerald!' exclaimed her dad. 'What in the underwater world are you doing out so late on your own? You're supposed to be at the sleepover!'

'I was,' sniffed Emerald. 'But I *really* needed plushie. You forgot to pack it!'

'*Oh*,' said her dad. 'I'm so sorry. I know you can't sleep without it! Sirena and I have just been so busy with . . . er . . .'

Emerald's dad glanced at the mermaid next to him—Sirena. She was friendly-looking with long, long hair and a starfish crown on her head. She was carrying a box in her arms, and now she glanced down at it as though unsure what to do.

'Um,' she said. 'Maybe we should go back to the house.'

'Good idea,' said Emerald's dad,

glancing at me. 'We can have a midnight
snack and you can introduce me to your
friend. She's got legs!'

Chapter FIVE

We all swam back to the house, and
Emerald's dad led us into the kitchen.
Emerald and I sat down on stools while he
made us some shrimp sandwiches with the
crusts cut off and two seaberry smoothie
drinks. Emerald looked the happiest I had
seen her all night as she chatted with her
dad and ate the midnight mermaid snacks.

She seemed completely different to how she had been earlier. Now I understood why Marina had invited her to the party. She *could* be really fun and friendly. I felt much less afraid of her now.

'Here's starfish plushie!' said Sirena, swimming into the room. She tossed it at Emerald and it floated through the water towards her. Emerald reached out her hands and grabbed it, hugging it to her chest.

'Thanks, Sirena,' she said, only a tiny bit grudgingly.

'I'm so sorry I forgot to put it in your bag,' said Emerald's dad. 'Sirena and I have been a bit distracted these past few days with . . . something.'

'I know,' replied Emerald, her face falling.

'Something for you,' said Emerald's dad.

'Me?!' said Emerald, her eyes lighting up again. 'I thought you had forgotten all about me!'

'Don't be silly!' said her dad. 'How could I ever forget about *you*?'

'Yes,' said Sirena. 'You've been the

only thing on our minds lately! We were planning a surprise for you to come home to tomorrow. But as you're here now, I wonder if . . .'

'. . . we ought to give it to you now instead!' finished Emerald's dad. 'We had to swim a long way to get it. That's why we're back so late tonight.'

'What is it?' asked Emerald. Her eyes narrowed, ever so slightly suspiciously. I could tell she still didn't trust her dad's new girlfriend.

'I'll go and get it,' said Sirena with a smile, and she disappeared from the kitchen for a moment, coming back with the box she had been carrying before in her arms.

'Here,' she said, putting it on the table.

Emerald stared at the box in wonder. It had lots of air holes or *waterholes* on the sides of it.

'Ooh!' I said, excited to see what was inside. 'What could it be, Emerald? Go on, open it!'

Emerald lifted the lid and peered inside. Her face broke into a smile SO big that I thought she might burst from happiness.

'Is it really for me?' she asked, staring at her dad as though she couldn't believe it.

'Of course it is!' said her dad. 'I know how much you've wanted a pet. I thought now might be the perfect time to get you one!'

Emerald put her hands into the box and lifted out something small and wriggly. It was an inky black octopus with little green fins on either side of its head, just like Emerald's!

'It's a girl octopus,' said Sirena. 'She's a very special rare sort. That's why we had to go so far to get her!'

The little octopus wriggled her

tentacles and swam up into the air,
bopping Emerald on the nose and then
swimming over to me and doing the same.
Emerald laughed.

'I love her so much already!' she said.

I reached out my hand and stroked the octopus's head. She felt so smooth and soft.

'I'm going to call her Inkibelle,' said Emerald. 'Thank you so much, Dad. And thank you . . . Sirena.'

Sirena smiled.

'Can I have a hug?' she asked shyly.

Emerald hesitated for a moment, and then she swished over to Sirena, wrapping her arms around her. I smiled, feeling happy for Emerald.

Emerald's dad looked at the clock on the wall.

'We really ought to be getting you two back to Marina's house,' he said. 'It's way past your bedtime!'

The four of us swam through the sea,
winding through the dark and silent
streets of Scallop City. When we arrived
back at Marina's house, Emerald slid the
window of Marina's bedroom back open.

'There's no point in waking anyone,'
she whispered. 'Isadora and I will just slip
inside and go to sleep.'

'OK,' said her dad. 'Well, Sirena and
I will see you tomorrow. We'll be here to
pick you up. Goodnight.'

He gave her a kiss and waved
goodbye to me. Then Emerald and I
floated back into Marina's bedroom,

closing the window behind us. We landed
softly on our spongy clamshell beds and
snuggled down under the covers. Emerald
sighed happily as she pulled both starfish
plushie and Inkibelle towards her, and
I squeezed Pink Rabbit tight. This time
I had no energy left for thinking scary
thoughts or missing Mum and Dad. I
closed my eyes and drifted straight off
to sleep.

Chapter SIX

By the time Emerald and I woke up the next morning, all the other merfriends were downstairs and having breakfast.

Emerald sat up in bed, yawning and stretching. She smiled at me. I smiled back, and we watched Inkibelle twist and twizzle in the water for a bit. She swam over to Pink Rabbit and bopped him on

the nose. Pink Rabbit bopped her back
with his paw.

'Thank you for coming with me last
night, Isadora,' said Emerald. 'It was
really kind of you. Especially as I was kind
of . . . moody yesterday.'

'That's OK,' I replied. 'It was fun to
see Scallop City at night!'

'It was,' agreed Emerald. 'And I feel so much better now! I think everything is going to be OK. But . . . I think I need to talk to Delphina before I do anything else. I wasn't very nice to her yesterday.'

'No,' I agreed.

'I was just feeling so sad and angry,' said Emerald. 'But maybe . . . it will be nice to have Delphina as my sister after all.'

Together we swam downstairs and into the kitchen.

'Hello, sleepyheads,' said Marina's mum. She peered at Inkibelle who was swimming by Emerald's ear.

'I don't remember seeing this little

octopus yesterday,' she said.

'Oh um . . . this is Inkibelle,' said
Emerald.

'Inkibelle?!' said Marina. 'She's so
cute! Where did you get her, Emerald?'

'Oh,' said Emerald. 'Well . . .' She
glanced at me and I shrugged, not
knowing whether Emerald wanted to tell
everyone about our midnight adventure
or not.

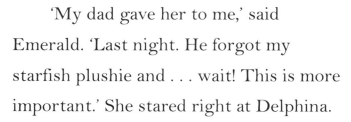

'My dad gave her to me,' said Emerald. 'Last night. He forgot my starfish plushie and . . . wait! This is more important.' She stared right at Delphina.

'I'm sorry for being mean to you yesterday,' she said. 'And lately.'

Delphina looked surprised. And then pleased. Her cheeks turned pink.

'Oh, it's OK,' she said. 'It's fine. We don't have to say we're sisters if you don't want to.'

'No, it's fine,' said Emerald. 'I mean, I guess I'll get used to it.'

'Really?' said Delphina, her whole face lighting up with delight.

'Of course!' said Emerald. 'I'll *try* my

best to be a good sister.'

Delphina nodded, getting up from
the table to hug Emerald. It made me feel
all warm inside, and I gave Pink Rabbit a
big squeeze.

After that, Emerald and I sat down. Together we told everyone the story of our midnight adventure.

'Ooh!' said Finn. 'I bet it was spooky swimming through Scallop City in the dark.'

'It was sort of spooky,' I said. 'But also very pretty and glowy!'

'I wish I could have come,' said Delphina.

'We'll go on an adventure another time,' Emerald said. 'I promise.'

Breakfast was . . . interesting. I had a slice of sand toast, which was very . . . gritty, and a glass of foamy sea milk. Afterwards, we all went back upstairs

to pack our things. I felt a bit sad that
Marina's party had almost come to an end,
but I was looking forward to seeing Mum
and Dad again. And to eating my usual
peanut butter on toast snack!

We waved goodbye to all the merfriends as one by one their parents came to pick them up. I gave Emerald an extra-special tight hug before she left.

'It was so nice to meet you!' I said. 'I hope we can meet again one day.'

'I hope so too,' said Emerald. 'Thanks for helping me last night, Isadora. You have a kind heart!'

'So do you!' I said, thinking back to how much Emerald had changed from the day before. She *did* have a kind heart. It had just taken me a little while to see it.

When all the merfriends had gone, it was time for Marina to take me back to the beach. We left her house and swam slowly through Scallop City. I tried to take in all the sights and sounds as we went so that I could remember them forever. Soon we were swimming away from all the mer-houses and into the wide ocean, the water getting shallower and shallower. When I saw sunlight piercing through the waves, I knew we were almost there. I swam towards the surface with Pink Rabbit in his bubble and burst out of the waves with Marina beside us.

'There's your mum and dad!' said
Marina, pointing to the little cove
where we had left them the day before.
They were sitting on a picnic rug with
Honeyblossom. When they saw Marina
and me swimming towards them they
jumped up, waving.

I swam closer to shore until it was shallow enough for my feet to touch the sand. Then I walked out of the water, dripping.

'Goodbye, Isadora!' said Marina, waving. 'I'm so glad you could come to my party!'

'I'm so glad I could too,' I said. 'Thank you for having me.'

We grinned at each other, and then Marina dipped her head back into the water, and with a splash of her tail, she was gone.

'We had better get you into some dry clothes,' said Mum, holding out her hand for me to take. 'Did you have a lovely time?'

'Tell us all about it!' said Dad. 'Did they have red juice under the water? Were there any vampire mermaids?'

I laughed.

'I didn't meet any vampire mermaids, Dad,' I replied. 'But I did meet a very gothic sort of mermaid. She had a sleek black octopus pet called Inkibelle. I think you'd have liked her style.'

'A sleek black octopus!' said Dad. 'I do like the sound of that.'

He took my other hand, and together we walked back to the picnic rug where Mum put Honeyblossom down.

'Hello little sister,' I said, kneeling down and giving her a big squish.

Then I changed into some lovely dry clothes that had been warmed by the sun. It felt so nice after having been underwater for so long. We all sat down, and Mum opened up a picnic hamper full of food, including my favourite—peanut butter sandwiches!

'I did enjoy my underwater adventure,' I said happily, as I took a bite of my sandwich. 'It was so much fun! But I'm glad to be back with you now. Sleeping under the sea is a bit . . . wet!'

Turn the page
for some
Isadorable
things to make
and do!

Make a shell necklace!

Next time you go to the beach, why not collect some shells and turn your favourite ones into a necklace?

Method:

1. Search for shells with holes in them.

2. Take the best ones home and wash thoroughly.

3. Thread on to a piece of string.

4.   If you would like to, add beads, pompoms, or any other decorations.

5.   Tie the two ends of the string together (making sure it's long enough to fit over your head!)

6.   Make some more for your friends!

How to make a shell crown

Isadora and her mermaid friends
have great fun making shell crowns.

Here's how to make your own.

What you will need:

★ Card

★ Shells (real or drawn)

★ Plastic gems, sequins, etc.

★ Scissors

★ Hole punch

★ Ribbon

★ PVA glue

Method:

1. Cut out a crown shape from the card, wide enough to cover your whole forehead.

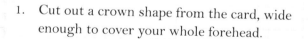

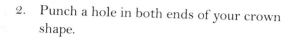

2. Punch a hole in both ends of your crown shape.

3. Thread a ribbon through each hole and tie a knot in the end to secure it.

4. Decorate your crown by gluing on shells, gems, and sequins.

5. Get a grown up to tie the ribbon at the back so that the crown fits on your head.

6. Enjoy feeling like mermaid royalty!

Things to spot at the beach!

Next time you go to the beach,
see which of these you can spot!

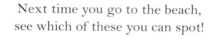

How to make seaberry cupcakes

Isadora eats some wonderful food at Marina's party—why not try these seaberry cupcakes? (Instead of seaberries, we've used cherries).

Ingredients
For the cakes:

★ 100g caster sugar
★ 100g butter, softened
★ 100g self-raising flour
★ 2 eggs
★ 1 tsp vanilla extract
★ Red food colouring

For the icing:

★ 200g butter, softened
★ 200g icing sugar
★ Sprinkles
★ A handful of glace cherries

Equipment:

- Weighing scales
- Bowl
- Sieve
- Whisk
- Fairy cake cases
- A 12-hole bun tin
- Piping bag
- A grown up helper

Method:

1. Preheat the oven to 180°C/Fan 160°C/gas 4.

2. Place fairy cake cases into a 12-hole bun tin.

3. Mix sugar and butter together in the bowl, then sift in the flour.

4. Add the eggs and vanilla extract.

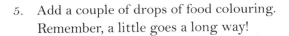

5. Add a couple of drops of food colouring. Remember, a little goes a long way!

6. Fill each paper case with the mixture.

7. Bake for 15–20 minutes or until the cakes are well risen and golden brown.

8. To make the icing, beat the butter and icing sugar together until well blended, then put in an icing bag.

9. Once the cakes are completely cool, pipe icing onto each cake and decorate.

10. Enjoy!

Spot the difference

It was a wonderful merfriends party.
Can you look closely and spot 5 differences
in these images?

Turn to page 122 for the answers!

If you met a mermaid, what kind of underwater adventure would you have?

Take the quiz to find out!

What kind of sea creature do you like best?

A. Shark

B. Whale

C. Clownfish

Which of these would you most like
to be when you grow up?

A. Explorer

B. Swimmer

C. Marine biologist

What do you like about the sea?

A. The crashing waves

B. How big it is

C. The beautiful fish and plants that are hidden underneath

Results

Mostly As

You love excitement, so your adventure would be a dramatic one involving shipwrecks, sharks, and a race to find lost treasure!

Mostly Bs

You are full of energy, so you would travel huge distances across the oceans, meeting lots of sea creatures from far and wide!

Mostly Cs

You love the beauty beneath the waves, so you would explore the coral reefs, learning all about their secrets and taking care of everything that lives there.

Wordsearch

Find the following hidden words!

ISADORA

EMERALD

PINK RABBIT

MERMAID

SHELL

SLEEPOVER

OCTOPUS

FISH

UNDERWATER

```
F  R  R  A  V  M  I  H  J  Z  O  S
B  M  F  S  H  E  L  L  N  E  P  E
N  P  C  L  Y  F  R  H  F  Q  J  N
P  I  M  E  M  E  R  A  L  D  A  N
U  N  D  E  R  W  A  T  E  R  Q  O
F  K  L  P  R  O  C  T  O  P  U  S
T  R  A  O  K  M  N  D  S  H  T  E
A  A  E  V  R  E  A  I  S  A  E  S
V  B  G  E  F  S  M  I  R  T  A  T
L  B  N  R  I  M  F  X  D  E  G  P
J  I  O  N  S  S  T  R  I  I  L  H
S  T  P  Z  H  H  Z  D  Y  F  C  I
```

Turn to page 122 for the answers!

Answers

```
F  R  R  A  V  M  I  H  J  Z  O  S
B  M  F  S  H  E  L  L  N  E  P  E
N  P  C  L  Y  F  R  H  F  Q  J  N
P  I  M  E  M  E  R  A  L  D  A  N
U  N  D  E  R  W  A  T  E  R  Q  O
F  K  L  P  R  O  C  T  O  P  U  S
T  R  A  O  K  M  N  D  S  H  T  E
A  A  E  V  R  E  A  I  S  A  E  S
V  B  G  E  F  S  M  I  R  T  A  T
L  B  N  R  I  M  F  X  D  E  G  P
J  I  O  N  S  S  T  R  I  I  L  H
S  T  P  Z  H  H  Z  D  Y  F  C  I
```

Do you know
in which book
Isadora first met
Marina . . . ?

Turn the page to find out!

ISADORA MOON

Goes Camping

Half vampire, half fairy, totally unique!

Harriet Muncaster

When Isadora loses her
dad's precious comb during a
trip to the beach, she knows
she has to get it back.
But when she goes looking
for it in the middle of the
night she finds more than
she was expecting . . .

Here's the moment
when Isadora and Marina
first meet, in this extract
from Isadora Moon
Goes Camping.

Pink Rabbit and I lay in the dark. I felt so
bad about the comb that I couldn't sleep.

It was lost forever at the bottom of
the deep blue sea!

Or was it?

I sat up in bed. Was there a chance
that the comb could have washed back up
on the sand?

I scrambled out of my sleeping bag and crawled towards the opening of our tent.

'Pink Rabbit!' I whispered. 'Wake up! We're going to the beach.'

Pink Rabbit bounced out of bed. I don't think he had been able to sleep either. Together we crept out of the tent and stood in the dark field. The sky was full of stars and all we could hear were the faint sounds of people snoring.

I tiptoed over to Mum and Dad's tent.

'We'll need Mum's wand for a torch,' I whispered to Pink Rabbit as I silently slid it out of her bag. I waved it in the air and the star immediately glowed pink. I reached down for Pink Rabbit's paw and together we flapped up into the air.

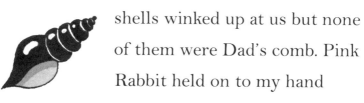 I love to fly, especially at night. We soared up high over the field until all the tents were just black little specks. Then we swooped down towards the beach and the sound of the roaring sea.

I pointed Mum's torch down at the sand.

'It might have washed up around here,' I said hopefully.

We walked up and down the shoreline, squinting in the pink wand-light. Little bits of sea glass and pearly shells winked up at us but none of them were Dad's comb. Pink Rabbit held on to my hand tightly. He finds the darkness a bit too mysterious sometimes.

Suddenly there came a small splashing sound from the sea.

I stared at Pink Rabbit.

'What was that?' I whispered.

Pink Rabbit didn't know because he had his paws over his eyes.

I peered out to sea. There was something shining and sparkling in the water. Maybe it was Dad's comb! I rose up into the air, pulling Pink Rabbit behind me.

'Come on!' I said to him. 'Let's look!'

We fluttered towards the shining thing in the sea. As we got closer I could see that it was moving. 'It can't be the

comb,' I said to Pink Rabbit. We flew a
little closer and heard a soft tinkly voice
calling out.

'Hello?'

I could see that there was a girl about my age in the sea. She had long, long hair and a gleaming fish tail that kept flicking in and out of the water. I hovered above her, holding Pink Rabbit clear of the waves.

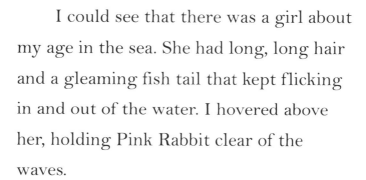

'Are you a mermaid?' I asked.

'Yes,' she said in a song-like voice. 'How are you floating up there?'

'I'm flying, not floating! I am half vampire, half fairy.' I turned in the air to show her my wings.

'I've never met a half vampire, half fairy before!' she said.

'I've never met a mermaid before!' I replied.

We both laughed. She had a laugh
that sounded like strings of shells tinkling
in the breeze.

'My name's Marina. What's yours?'

'Isadora,' I said. Then I pointed at
Pink Rabbit. 'This is Pink Rabbit.'

'He's funny,' she giggled, reaching out
and poking his stomach.

Pink Rabbit stiffened. He doesn't like
to be called funny.

'What are you doing out here so late
at night?' Marina asked.

'I was looking for something really
precious. It got lost here today while we
were at the beach.'

'Oh?' Marina said. 'What is it?'

'A comb,' I said. 'A really special comb. It's my dad's.'

'Was it black?' Marina asked. 'With twirly designs on it? And rubies?'

'Yes!' I said hopefully. 'Have you seen it?!'

'I have…' said Marina, 'but…'

'Where is it?' I asked excitedly. 'I need it back!'

Marina looked a bit worried.

'The Mermaid Princess has it,' she said. 'All the nicest jewels found on the beach always go to the Mermaid Princess. She doesn't like to share.'

'But it's my dad's comb,' I said in a panicky voice. 'I need it back.' I felt my eyes fill with tears.

Marina bit her lip. 'It's a bit tricky,' she said. 'There are different rules for under the sea you know. It's finders keepers here.'

I wiped my eyes and sniffed.

'I'll tell you what,' said Marina. 'Why don't I take you to the Mermaid Princess? You can ask her yourself! Maybe she'll let you have it back if you explain.'

Harriet Muncaster

Harriet Muncaster, that's me! I'm the
author and illustrator of Isadora Moon.
Yes really! I love anything teeny tiny,
anything starry, and everything glittery.

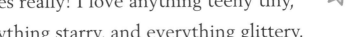

Many more magical stories to collect!

Goes to School

Goes Camping

Goes to the Ballet

Has a Birthday

ISADORA MOON

Gets in Trouble

Half vampire, half fairy, totally unique!

Harriet Muncaster

ISADORA MOON

Goes on a School Trip

Half vampire, half fairy, totally unique!

Harriet Muncaster

ISADORA MOON

Goes to the Fair

Half vampire, half fairy, totally unique!

Harriet Muncaster

ISADORA MOON

Makes Winter Magic

Half vampire, half fairy, totally unique!

Harriet Muncaster

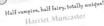

ISADORA MOON
Has a Sleepover

Half vampire, half fairy, totally unique!
Harriet Muncaster

ISADORA MOON
Puts on a Show

Half vampire, half fairy, totally unique!
Harriet Muncaster

ISADORA MOON
Goes on Holiday

Half vampire, half fairy, totally unique!
Harriet Muncaster

ISADORA MOON
Goes to a Wedding

Half vampire, half fairy, totally unique!
Harriet Muncaster

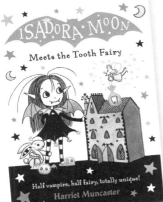

ISADORA MOON
Meets the Tooth Fairy
Half vampire, half fairy, totally unique!
Harriet Muncaster

ISADORA MOON
and the Shooting Star
Half vampire, half fairy, totally unique!
Harriet Muncaster

ISADORA MOON
Gets the Magic Pox
Half vampire, half fairy, totally unique!
Harriet Muncaster

MIRABELLE

Meet Isadora's naughty cousin,
Mirabelle Starspell, in her very own stories.

From the world of ISADORA MOON

MIRABELLE
Gets up to Mischief

Half witch, half fairy, totally naughty!
Harriet Muncaster

From the world of ISADORA MOON

MIRABELLE
Breaks the Rules

Half witch, half fairy, totally naughty!
Harriet Muncaster

From the world of ISADORA MOON
MIRABELLE
Has a Bad Day
Half witch, half fairy, totally naughty!
Harriet Muncaster

From the world of ISADORA MOON
MIRABELLE
in Double Trouble
Half witch, half fairy, totally naughty!
Harriet Muncaster

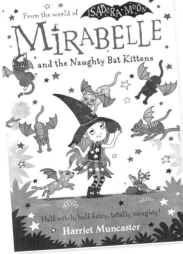

From the world of ISADORA MOON
MIRABELLE
and the Naughty Bat Kittens
Half witch, half fairy, totally naughty!
Harriet Muncaster

From the world of ISADORA MOON
MIRABELLE
and the Magical Mayhem
Half witch, half fairy, totally naughty!
Harriet Muncaster